PYTHON

A COMPLETE PRACTICAL SOLUTION

DR. EKATA GUPTA

I dedicate this book to my family and friends who have always been the support for me .

Contents

CHAPTER ONE

Beginner Level Questions

1. **Write a program to accept two integers and print their sum.**

```
num1=int(input("Enter 1st Number: "))
num2=int(input("Enter 2nd Number: "))
print("Sum of  two number is ",num1+num2)
```

```
Enter 1st Number: 8
Enter 2nd Number: 4
Sum of  two number is  12
```

Solution to Question 1

2. **Write a program that accepts the radius of a circle and prints it's area.**

```
import math
radius=int(input("Enter Radius of a circle "))
area=math.pi*radius*radius
print(area)
```

```
Enter Radius of a circle 5
78.53981633974483
```

Solution to Question 2

3. **Write a program that accepts base and height and calculate the area of a triangle.**

```
base=int(input("Enter Base of a Triangle: "))
height=int(input("Enter Height of a Triangle: "))
area=(base*height)/2
print("Area of a Triangle is ",area)
```

```
Enter Base of a Triangle: 5
Enter Height of a Triangle: 6
Area of a Triangle is  15.0
```

Solution to Question 3

4. **Write a program that inputs a student's marks in three subjects (out of 100) and prints the percentage marks.**

```
sub1=int(input("Enter Marks of Subject 1 (Out of 100) : "))
sub2=int(input("Enter Marks of Subject 2 (Out of 100) : "))
sub3=int(input("Enter Marks of Subject 3 (Out of 100) : "))
percentage=((sub1+sub2+sub3)/300)*100
print("Percentage = ",percentage)
```

```
Enter Marks of Subject 1 (Out of 100) : 85
Enter Marks of Subject 2 (Out of 100) : 88
Enter Marks of Subject 3 (Out of 100) : 86
Percentage =  86.33333333333333
```

Solution to Question 4

5. **Write a program to compute the area of square and triangle.**

```
s=int(input("enter side of square="))
a,b=map(int,input(' enter the base and height of triangle=').split())
print('area of square is = ',s*s)
print('area of triangle is',0.5*a*b)
```

```
enter side of square=5
 enter the base and height of triangle=6 7
area of square is =  25
area of triangle is 21.0
```

Solution to question 5

6. **Write a program to calculate simple interest.**

```
a,b,c=map(int,input('enter principle,rate and time ').split())
print((a*b*c)/100)
```

```
enter principle,rate and time 5 6 7
2.1
```

Solution to Question 6

7. **Write a program to read two numbers and prints their quotient and reminder.**

```
a,b=map(int,input().split())
print(a//b,a%b)
```

```
5 9
0 5
```

Solution to Question 7

8. **Write a program to find whether a given number is even or odd.**

```
x=lambda i:'even' if i%2==0 else 'odd'
x(12),x(5)
```

```
('even', 'odd')
```

Solution to Question 8

9. **Write a program to find the largest among the three integers.**

```
max(list(map(int,input().split())))
```

```
5 4 6 22 25

25
```

Solution to Question 9

10. **Write a program to find the lowest among the three integers.**

```
min(list(map(int,input().split())))
```

```
64 56 7 8 3 32

3
```

Solution to Question 10

11. **Write a program that accepts the length and breadth of the rectangle and calculate its area.**

```
l,b=map(int,input('enter length and breath').split())
print(l*b)
```

```
enter length and breath5 9
45
```

Solutiont o Question 11

12. **Write a program that accepts weight in Kg and height in meters and calculate the BMI.**

```
w=int(input('enter weight '))
h=eval(input('enter height '))
bmi=w/(h**2)
print(bmi)
```

```
enter weight 70
enter height 1.24
45.525494276795
```

Solution to Question 12

13. **Write a program that reads the number n and print the value of n^2, n^3 and n^4.**

```
n=int(input())
for i in range(2,5):
    print(n**i,end=" ")
```

```
5
25 125 625
```

Solution to Question 13

14. **Write a program to accept the marks of five subjects and calculate the average marks.**

```
l=list(map(int,input('enter marks of 5 subjects').split()))
print(sum(l)/len(l))
```

```
enter marks of 5 subjects56 89 78 45 98
73.2
```

Solution to Question 14

15. **Write a program to accept the height in cm and convert it into feet and inches.**

```
h=eval(input('enter height in cm '))
print('in feets ',h/30.48)
print('in inches ',h/2.54)
```

```
enter height in cm 360
in feets  11.811023622047244
in inches  141.73228346456693
```

Solution to Question 15

16. **Write a program that accepts the age and print if one is eligible to vote or not.**

```
a=int(input('enter age'))
if a>=18:
    print('eligible to vote')
else:
    print('not eligible to vote')
```

```
enter age16
not eligible to vote
```

Solution to Question 16

17. **Write a program that accepts two numbers and check if the first number is fully divisible by the second number or not.**

```
a,b=map(int,input().split())
if a%b==0:
    print('yes fully divisible')
else:
    print('not fully divisible')
```

```
8 4
yes fully divisible
```

Solution to Question 17

18. **Write a program to read base, width and height of parallelogram and calculate its area and perimeter.**

```
a,b,c=map(int,input('enter base,width and height').split())
print('perimeter: ',2*(a+b))
print('area: ',a*c)
```

```
enter base,width and height12 4 56
perimeter:  32
area:  672
```

Solution to Question 18

19. **Write a program to accept the year and check if it is a leap year or not.**

```
n=int(input('enter year'))
if n%4==0 and (not(n%100==0) or n%400==0):
    print('leap year')
else:
    print('not a leap year')
```

```
enter year2010
not a leap year
```

Solution to Question 19

20. **Write a program to obtain x, y, z and calculate $4x^4+3y^3+9z+6\pi$.**

```
x,y,z=map(int,input().split())
a=4*x**4
b=(3*y**3)
c=9*z
d=(6*3.14)
print(a+b+c+d)
```

```
6 8 4
6774.84
```

Solution to Question 20

21. **Write a program to input a number and print its square if it is odd, otherwise print its square root.**

```
n=int(input())
if n%2==0:
    print(n**0.5)
else:
    print(n**2)
```

```
44
6.6332495807108
```

Solution to Question 21

22. **Write a program to input a number and check whether it is positive, negative or zero.**

```
n=int(input())
if n==0:
    print('zero')
elif n<0:
    print('negative')
else:
    print('positive')
```

```
-12
negative
```

Solution to question 22

23. **Write a program to input percentage marks of a student and find the grade as per the following criterion:**

Marks	Grade
>=90	A
75-90	B
60-75	C
Below 60	D

```
n=int(input())
if n>=90:
    print("A")
elif n>75 and n<90:
    print("B")
elif n>60 and n<75:
    print("C")
else:
    print("D")
```

```
59
D
```

Solution to Question 23

24. Write a program to enter a number and check if it is a prime number or not.

```
n=int(input())
c=0
for i in range(1,n+1):
    if n%i==0:
        c+=1
if c==2:
    print('prime')
else:
    print('composite')
```

```
23
prime
```

Solution to Question 24

25. Write a program to display a menu for calculating the area of the circle or perimeter of the circle.

```
r=eval(input('enter radius'))
print('perimeter: ',3.14*2*r)
print('area: ',3.14*r*r)
```

```
enter radius25
perimeter:  157.0
area:  1962.5
```

Solution to Question 25

26.Write a program that reads two numbers and an arithmetic operator and displays the computed result.

```
a,b=map(int,input().split())
s=input()
if s=='+':
    print(a+b)
elif s=='-':
    print(a-b)
elif s=='*':
    print(a*b)
elif s=='/':
    print(a/b)
```

```
2 25
+
27
```

Solution to Question 26

27. **Write a program to print whether a given character is an uppercase or a lowercase character or a digit or any other character.**

```
s=input()
if s.isupper():
    print('uppercase')
if s.islower():
    print('lowercase')
if s.isdigit():
    print('digit')
if not s.isalnum():
    print('special character')
```

```
5
digit
```

Solution to Question 27

28. Write a program to calculate and print the roots of a quadratic equation $ax^2+bx+c=0.(a\neq0)$

```
a,b,c=map(int,input().split())
x=-b+((b**2-(4*a*c))**0.5)/(2*a)
y=-b-((b**2-(4*a*c))**0.5)/(2*a)
print(x,y)
```

```
12 3 6
(-3+0.6959705453537528j) (-3-0.6959705453537528j)
```

Solution to Question 28

29.Write a program to print the sum of natural numbers between 1 to 7. Print the sum progressively i.e. after adding each natural number, a print sum so far.

```
c=0
for i in range(1,7):
    c+=i
print(c)
```

```
21
```

Solution to Question 29

30. Write a program to calculate the factorial of a number.

```
n=int(input())
c=1
for i in range(1,n+1):
    c*=i
print(c)
```

```
3
6
```

Solution to Question 30

31. Write a program to create a triangle of stars using a nested loop.

```
n=int(input())
for i in range(1,n+1):
    #for j in i:
    print('*'*i,end="")
    print("")
```

```
5
*
**
***
****
*****
```

Solution to Question 31

32. Write a Python script to print Fibonacci series' first 20 elements.

```
a=-1
b=1
for i in range(20):
    c=a+b
    a,b=b,c
    print(c,end=" ")
```

```
0 1 1 2 3 5 8 13 21 34 55 89 144 233 377 610 987 1597 2584 4181
```

Solution to Question 32

33.Write a program to read an integer>1000 and reverse the number.

```
n=int(input())
if n>1000:
    print(str(n)[::-1])
```

```
2456
6542
```

Solution to Question 33

34.Input three angles and determine if they form a triangle or not.

```
a,b,c=map(int,input().split())
if a+b+c==180:
    print('form a triangle')
else:
    print('does not forms a triangle' )
```

```
112 54 98
does not forms a triangle
```

Solution to Question 34

35. Write a Python script that displays the first ten Mersenne numbers.

```
for i in range(1,11):
    print((2**i)-1,end=" ")
```

```
1 3 7 15 31 63 127 255 511 1023
```

Solution to Question 35

36.Write a Python script that displays the first ten Mersenne numbers and displays 'Prime' next to Mersenne Prime Numbers.

```
for i in range(1,11):
    x=(2**i)-1
    c=0
    for j in range(1,x+1):
        if x%j==0:
            c+=1
    if c==2:
        print(x,'prime')
    else:
        print(x)
```

```
1
3 prime
7 prime
15
31 prime
63
127 prime
255
511
1023
```

Solution to Question 36

37. Write a program to calculate BMI and print the nutritional status as per the following table:

Nutritional Status WHO criteria BMI

cut-off

Underweight <18.5
Normal 18.5-24.9
Overweight 25-29.9
Obese ≥30

```
w=int(input('enter weight '))
h=eval(input('enter height '))
bmi=w/(h**2)
if bmi<18.5:
    print('underweight')
if bmi>18.5 and bmi<24.9:
    print('normal')
if bmi>25 and bmi<29.9:
    print('overweight')
if bmi>=30:
    print('obese')
```

```
enter weight 80
enter height 5.7
underweight
```

Solution to Question 37

38. Write a python script to print the following pattern.

1
1 3
1 3 5
1 3 5 7

```
for i in range(1,5):
    for j in range(1,i+1):
        print((2*j)-1,end=' ')
    print('')
```

```
1
1 3
1 3 5
1 3 5 7
```

Solutiont to Question 38

39. Write a program to find the sum of the series : $s=1+x+x^{2}+x^{3}+x^{4}...+x^{n}$

```
n=int(input())
x=int(input())
s=1
for i in range(2,n+1):
    s+=x**i
print(s)
```

```
5
2
61
```

Solution to Question 39

40. Write a python script to input two numbers and print their LCM and HCF.

```
a,b=map(int,input('enter 2 no. ').split())
for i in range(1,min([a,b])+1):
    if a%i==0 and b%i==0:
        hcf=i
lcm=a*b//i
print('hcf: ',hcf)
print('lcm: ',lcm)
```

```
enter 2 no. 34 6
hcf:  2
lcm:  34
```

Solution to Question 40

41. Write a python script to calculate the sum of the following series:

S=(1)+(1+2)+(1+2+3)+......+(1+2+3+....+n)

```
n=int(input())
s=0
for i in range(1,n+1):
    for j in range(1,i+1):
        s+=j
print(s)
```

```
3
10
```

Solution to Question 41

42. Write a program to print the following using a single loop (no nested loops)

1

1 1

1 1 1

1 1 1 1

1 1 1 1 1

```
for i in range(6):
    print('1 '*i)
```

```
1
1 1
1 1 1
1 1 1 1
1 1 1 1 1
```

Solution to Question 42

43. Write a program to print a pattern like:

4 3 2 1

4 3 2

4 3

4

```
#43
r=int(input("Enter Number of Rows: "))
i=-1
for l in range(r,0,-1):
    i+=1
    for k in range(r,i,-1):
        print(k," ",end="")
    print()
```

```
Enter Number of Rows: 4
4  3  2  1
4  3  2
4  3
4
```

Solution to Question 43

CHAPTER TWO

Basic Level Questions

1. **To find the sum of first n natural numbers, where n is to be input from the user.**

```
#Q1
n=int(input("Enter no.:"))
s=0
for i in range(n+1):
    s+=i
print("Sum of first",n,"natural numbers:",s)
```

```
Enter no.:5
Sum of first 5 natural numbers: 15
```

Solution to Question 1

2. **To input a number and display its first 10 multiples.**

```
#Q2
n=int(input("Enter no.:"))
for i in range(1,11):
    print(n*i)
```

```
Enter no.:5
5
10
15
20
25
30
35
40
45
50
```

Solution to Question2

3. **To input an integer and find the sum of its digits**

```
#Q3
n=int(input("Enter a number:"))
tot=0
while(n>0):
    dig=n%10
    tot=tot+dig
    n=n//10
print("The total sum of digits is:",tot)
```

```
Enter a number:1892
The total sum of digits is: 20
```

Solution to Question 3

4. **To input an integer and check whether it is prime or not.**

```
#Q4
n=int(input("Enter no.:"))
c=0
for i in range(1,n+1):
    if n%i==0:
        c+=1
if c==2:
    print('prime')
else:
    print('Not a prime')
```

```
Enter no.:3
prime
```

Solution to Question 4

5. **To find the sum of first n even natural numbers, where n is to be input from the user.**

```
#Q5
n=int(input("Enter no.:"))
s=0
for i in range(n+1):
    if i%2==0:
        s+=i
print("Sum of first",n,"even natural numbers:",s)
```

```
Enter no.:9
Sum of first 9 even natural numbers: 20
```

Solution to Question 5

6. **To input an integer and find its factorial. Factorial of an integer n (n>=1), is defined as the product of all natural numbers from 1 to n, and is represented by n!. For example, factorial of 5 is represented by 5! and is equal to 120 (=1x2x3x4x5).Factorial of 0 is defined as 1 and factorial of negative integers is not defined.**

```
#Q6
n=int(input("Enter no.:"))
m=1
for i in range(1,n+1):
    m*=i

if n<0:
    print('negative integer')
else:
    print("Factorial",m)
```

```
Enter no.:6
Factorial 720
```

Solution to Question 6

7. **Write script to input a number. If the number is negative, then again input the number. Keep on doing so until the user enters a non-negative (zero or positive) number. When the user enters a non-negative number, display the message "Thank you".**

```
#Q7
n=int(input("Enter no.:"))
while(n<0):
    n=int(input())
if n>0:
    print('thank you')
```

```
Enter no.:5
thank you
```

Solution to Question 7

8. . **Write script to input 10 numbers and then display the largest and second largest of the numbers entered.**

```
#Q8
l=list(set(map(int,input("Enter 10 no.:").split())))
print("FIrst Largest no.:",max(l))
print("Second largest number:",l[-2])
```

```
Enter 10 no.:1 2 8 4 5 7 2 9 3 10
FIrst Largest no.: 10
Second largest number: 9
```

Solution to Question 8

9. . **Write script to input a list of n number and count how many of the entered numbers were prime.**

```
#Q9
l=list(map(int,input("Enter numbers:").split()))
x=[]
for i in range(len(l)):
    c=0
    for j in range(1,l[i]+1):
        if l[i]%j==0:
            c+=1
    if c==2:
        x.append(l[i])
print("Prime numbers are:",*x,sep='\n')
```

```
Enter numbers:1 2 3 4 5 6 7 8 9 10
Prime numbers are:
2
3
5
7
```

Solution to Question 9

10. **To input an integer and find the product of its odd digits. If the number does not contain any odd digit, then the program should display an appropriate message instead of the product.**

```
n=int(input("Enter the Integer : "))
m=1
for i in str(n):
    if int(i)%2!=0:
        m*=int(i)
if m==1:
    print('come on, add some odd integers :( ')
else:
    print(m)
```

```
Enter the Integer : 1259
45
```

Solution to Question 10

CHAPTER THREE

String Slicing

1.Program to get a string made of the first 2 and last 2 characters. If string length is less than 2, return instead of the empty string.

```
def string_both_ends(str):
    if len(str)<2:
        return ''

    return str[0:2]+str[-2:]

print(string_both_ends('rajat'))
print(string_both_ends('ch'))
print(string_both_ends('c'))
```

```
raat
chch
```

Solution to question 1

2. Program to get a single string from two given strings, separated by space and swap the first two characters of each string.

```
#Q2
def chars_mix_up(a, b):
    new_a = b[:2] + a[2:]
    new_b = a[:2] + b[2:]

    return new_a + ' ' + new_b
print(chars_mix_up('abc', 'xyz'))
```

```
xyc abz
```

Solution to Question 2

3. Program to add "ing" at the end of string. If string already ends with "ing" then add "ly" instead.

```
#Q3
def add_string(str1):
    length = len(str1)

    if length > 2:
        if str1[-3:] == 'ing':
            str1 += 'ly'
        else:
            str1 += 'ing'

    return str1
print(add_string('ab'))
print(add_string('abc'))
print(add_string('string'))
```

```
ab
abcing
stringly
```

Solution to Question 3

4. Program to find the length of a string taken from the user without using len function.

```
#Q4
string=input("Enter string:")
count=0
for i in string:
      count=count+1
print("Length of the string is:",count)
```

```
Enter string:Shagun
Length of the string is: 6
```

Solution to Question 4

5. Program to check if the letter "e" is present in the word "Umbrella".

```
#Q5
s="Umbrella"
print("e" in s)
```

```
True
```

Solution to Question 5

6. Program to find the number of vowels, consonants, digits and white space characters in a string.

```
#Q6
def countCharacterType(str):

    vowels = 0
    consonant = 0
    specialChar = 0
    digit - 0

    for i in range(0, len(str)):

        ch - str[i]

        if ( (ch >= 'a' and ch <= 'z') or
             (ch >= 'A' and ch <= 'Z') ):

            # To handle upper case letters
            ch - ch.lower()

            if (ch == 'a' or ch == 'e' or ch == 'i'
                        or ch == 'o' or ch == 'u'):
                vowels += 1
            else:
                consonant += 1

        elif (ch >= '0' and ch <= '9'):
            digit +- 1
        else:
            specialChar += 1

    print("Vowels:", vowels)
    print("Consonant:", consonant)
    print("Digit:", digit)
    print("Special Character:", specialChar)

str = "Welcome to my world"
countCharacterType(str)
```

```
Vowels: 5
Consonant: 11
Digit: 0
Special Character: 3
```

Solution to Question 6

7. Capitalize every vowel of the string.

```
#Q7
str=input("Enter a string:")
new_str=""
for i in str:
    if i=='a' or i=='e' or i=='i' or i=='o' or i=='u':
        new_str=new_str+i.upper()
    else:
        new_str=new_str+i
print(new_str)
```

```
Enter a string:Shagun
ShAgUn
```

Solution to Question 7

8. Write a program that reads a string and then prints a string that capitalizes every other letter in the string

```
x=input()
s=''
for i in range(len(x)):
    if i%2==0:
        s+=x[i].lower()
    else:
        s+=x[i].upper()
print(s)
```

```
rajat ahlawat
rAjAt aHlAwAt
```

Solution to Question 8

9. Program to check if the word 'orange' is present in the "This is orange juice".

```
#Q9
a = "This is orange juice"
print ('orange' in a.split())
```

```
True
```

Solution to Question 9

10. Capitalize the last character of every word in the string.

```
#Q10
String = input('Enter the String :')
String = String[0:1] + String[1:len(String)-1] + String[len(String)-1:len(String)].upper()
print(String)
```

```
Enter the String :Shagun
ShaguN
```

Solution to Question 10

11. Program to make a new string with all the consonants deleted from the string "Hello, have a good day".

```
#Q11
a = ['a','e','i','o','u','A','E','I','O','U',' ']
b = "Hello, have a good day"
for i in b:
    if i not in a:
        b = b[:b.index(i)]+b[b.index(i)+1:]
print (b)
```

```
eo ae a oo a
```

Solution to Question11

12. A program that reads a line and prints its statistics like:

The number of uppercase letters:

The number of lowercase letters:

The number of alphabets:

The number of digits:

```
s=input()
l=0
u=0
a=0
d=0
for i in range(len(s)):
    if s[i].islower():
        l+=1
    if s[i].isupper():
        u+=1
    if s[i].isalpha():
        a+=1
    if s[i].isdigit():
        d+=1
print('lowercases: ',l)
print('uppercases: ',u)
print('alphabets: ',a)
print('digit: ',d)
```

```
sjdbhaJSBjfsf  FJSFH sfjhsaf54695
lowercases:  17
uppercases:  8
alphabets:  25
digit:  5
```

Solution to Question 12

13. Write a program that reads a line and a substring and displays the number of occurrences of the given substring in the line.

```
n=input()
a=input()
s=set()
for i in range(len(n)):
    x=n.find(a,i)

    if x==-1:
        break
    else:
        s.add(x)
print(len(s))
```

```
abcdcdcdcdc
cdc
4
```

Solution to Question 13

14. Write a program that takes a string with multiple words and then capitalizes the first letter of each word and forms a new string out of it.

```
s=input()
s=s.capitalize()
r=''
l=[]
l.extend(s)
x=set()
for i in range(len(l)):
    t=l.count(' ')
    a=l.index(' ',i)
    x.add(a)
    if len(x)==t:
        break
for i in range(len(l)):
    for j in x:

        q=l.pop(j+1)
        l.insert(j+1,q.upper())
for i in range(len(l)):
    r+=l[i]
print(r)
```

```
hello  world   lol
Hello  World   Lol
```

Solution to Question 14

15. Write a program that reads a string and checks whether it is a palindrome string

```
s=int(input())
if s==int(str(s)[::-1]):
    print('its palindrone')
else:
    print('not a pallindrone')
```

```
121
its palindrone
```

Solution to Question 15

16. Write a program that reads a string and displays the longest substring of the given string having just the consonants

```
a=input()
r=''
s=['a','e','i','o','u']
for i in range(len(a)):
    if a[i] not in s:
        r+=a[i]
print(r)
```

```
hbuyuubuf uygugy iughuyg
hbybf yggy ghyg
```

Solution to Question 16

17. Write a program that reads the email id of a person in the form of a string and ensures that it belongs

to domain @edupillar.com (Assumption: no invalid characters are there in email-id)

```
s=input('enter email id ')
if s=='domain@edupillar.com':
    print('valid')
else:
    prnt('not valid')
```

```
enter email id domain@edupillar.com
valid
```

Solution to Question 17

CHAPTER FOUR

List

1. **WAP to remove all odd numbers from the given list**

```
l=list(map(int,input().split()))
for i in l:
    if i%2!=0:
        l.remove(i)
print(l)
```

```
1 2 3 4 5 6 7 8 9
[2, 4, 6, 8]
```

Solution to Question 1

2. **WAP to display the second largest element of a given list.**

```
sorted(set(map(int,input().split())))[-2]
```

```
2 3 3 4 5 6 7 7 9

7
```

Solution to Question 2

3.WAP to display frequencies of all the elements of a list.

```
l=list(map(int,input().split()))
d={}
for i in range(len(l)):
    d[l[i]]=l.count(l[i])
print(d)
```

```
1 1 2 3 3 4 4 5 5 6 6 7 7 7 6 5 5 7 8 9
{1: 2, 2: 1, 3: 2, 4: 2, 5: 4, 6: 3, 7: 4, 8: 1, 9: 1}
```

Solution to Question 3

4. WAP in Python to find and display the sum of all the values which are ending with 3 from a list.

```
l=list(map(int,input().split()))
s=0
for i in l:
    if str(i)[-1]=='3':
        print(i)
        s+=i
print(s)
```

```
3 1 123 4 56 33
3
123
33
159
```

Solution to question 4

5. WAP to search an element from the given list.

```
l=list(map(int,input().split()))
n=int(input())
x=False
for i in l:
    if n==i:
        x=True
if x:
    print('element found')
else:
    print('element not found')
```

```
1 2 32 4 5 67
5
element found
```

Solution to question 5

6. Program to demonstrate the slice operations used to access the elements of the list

```
num_list=[1,2,3,4,5,6,7,8,9,10]
print("num_list is :" ,num_list)
print("first element in the lsit is ",num_list[0])
print("num_list[2:5]= ", num_list[2:5])
print("num_list[::2] = " ,num_list[::2])
print("num_list[1::3] = " ,num_list[1::3])
```

```
num_list is : [1, 2, 3, 4, 5, 6, 7, 8, 9, 10]
first element in the lsit is  1
num_list[2:5]=  [3, 4, 5]
num_list[::2] =  [1, 3, 5, 7, 9]
num_list[1::3] =  [2, 5, 8]
```

Solution to Question 6

7. Program to illustrate deletion of numbers froma list using del statements

```
num_list=[1,2,3,4,5,6,7,8,9,10]
del num_list[2:4]
print(num_list)

[1, 2, 5, 6, 7, 8, 9, 10]
```

Solution to Question 7

8. Program to insert a list in another list using the slice operation

```
num_list=[1,9,11,13,15]
print("original list :" ,num_list)
num_list[2]=[3,5,7]
print("after inserting another list , the updated list is :" ,num_list)

original list : [1, 9, 11, 13, 15]
after inserting another list , the updated list is : [1, 9, [3, 5, 7], 13, 15]
```

Solution to Question 8

9. Program to illustrate nested list

```
list1=[1,'a',"abc",[2,3,4,5],8.9]
i=0
while i< (len(list1)):
  print("List1[",i,"] = " , list1[i])
  i+=1

List1[ 0 ] =  1
List1[ 1 ] =  a
List1[ 2 ] =  abc
List1[ 3 ] =  [2, 3, 4, 5]
List1[ 4 ] =  8.9
```

Solution to Question 9

10. Program to create a copy as well as the clone othe original list

```
list1=[1,2,3,4,5,6,7,8,9,10]
list2=list1
print("List1 = ",list1)
print("List2 = ",list2)
list3=list1[2:6]
print("list3 = " ,list3)

List1 =  [1, 2, 3, 4, 5, 6, 7, 8, 9, 10]
List2 =  [1, 2, 3, 4, 5, 6, 7, 8, 9, 10]
list3 =  [3, 4, 5, 6]
```

Solution to Question 10

CHAPTER FIVE

Tuples

1.WAP to accept values from user and create a tuple.

```
t=tuple(map(int,input().split()))
print(t)
```

```
1 2 3 4 5
(1, 2, 3, 4, 5)
```

Solution to Question 1

2. Write a Python program to remove an item from a tuple

```
t=tuple(map(int,input().split()))
x=t[-1]
a=list(t)
a.remove(x)
print(tuple(a))
```

```
1 2 3 4 5
(1, 2, 3, 4)
```

Solution to Question 2

3.Write a program to input n numbers from the user. Store these numbers in a tuple. Print the maximum, minimum, sum and mean of number from this tuple.

```
t=tuple(map(int,input().split()))
print(max(t))
print(min(t))
print(sum(t))
print(sum(t)/len(t))
```

```
1 2 3 4 5 6 7
7
1
28
4.0
```

Solution to Question 3

4. Reverse the tuple

```
tuple1 = (10, 20, 30, 40, 50)
tuple1 = tuple1[::-1]
print(tuple1)

(50, 40, 30, 20, 10)
```

Solution to Question 4

5. The given tuple is a nested tuple. write a Python program to print the value 20.

Given:

tuple1 = ("Orange", [10, 20, 30], (5, 15, 25))

```
tuple1 = ("Orange", [10, 20, 30], (5, 15, 25))

# understand indexing
# tuple1[0] = 'Orange'
# tuple1[1] = [10, 20, 30]
# list1[1][1] = 20

print(tuple1[1][1])

20
```

Solution to Question 5

6. Sort a tuple of tuples by 2nd item
Given:
tuple1 = ((‘a’, 23),(‘b’, 37),(‘c’, 11), (’d',29))

```
tuple1 = (('a', 23), ('b', 37), ('c', 11), ('d', 29))
tuple1 = tuple(sorted(list(tuple1), key=lambda x: x[1]))
print(tuple1)

(('c', 11), ('a', 23), ('d', 29), ('b', 37))
```

Solution to Question 6

CHAPTER SIX

Dictionary

1.Write a program to input the total number of sections and stream name in 11th class and display all information on the output screen

```
n=int(input())
d={}
for i in range(n):
    d[chr(65+i)]=input()
print(d)
```

```
3
science
commerce
arts
{'A': 'science', 'B': 'commerce', 'C': 'arts'}
```

Solution to Question 1

2.WAP to store students' details like admission number, roll number, name and percentage in a dictionary and display information on the basis of admission number.

```
n=int(input())
d={}
for i in range(n):

    d[input('admission no. ')]=list(map(str,input('enter rollno,name,percentage'
print(d)
```

```
2
enter rollno,name,percentage1 thor 98
admission no. 1000
enter rollno,name,percentage2 loki
admission no. 1001
{'1000': ['1', 'thor', '98'], '1001': ['2', 'loki']}
```

Solution to Question 2

3. Write a Python program to sort (ascending and descending) a dictionary by value

```
import operator
d = {1: 2, 3: 4, 4: 3, 2: 1, 0: 0}
print('Original dictionary : ',d)
sorted_d = sorted(d.items(), key=operator.itemgetter(1))
print('Dictionary in ascending order by value : ',sorted_d)
sorted_d = dict( sorted(d.items(), key=operator.itemgetter(1),reverse=True))
print('Dictionary in descending order by value : ',sorted_d)
```

```
Original dictionary :  {1: 2, 3: 4, 4: 3, 2: 1, 0: 0}
Dictionary in ascending order by value :  [(0, 0), (2, 1), (1, 2), (4, 3), (3, 4)]
Dictionary in descending order by value :  {3: 4, 4: 3, 1: 2, 2: 1, 0: 0}
```

Solution to Question 3

4. Write a Python script to merge two Python dictionaries.

```
d1 = {'car1': 100, 'car2': 200}
d2 = {'bus1': 300, 'bus2': 200}
d = d1.copy()
d.update(d2)
print(d)
```

```
{'car1': 100, 'car2': 200, 'bus1': 300, 'bus2': 200}
```

Solution to Question 4

5. Write a Python program to sum all the items in a dictionary.

```
my_dict = {'d1':1050,'d2':-154,'d3':2407}
print(sum(my_dict.values()))
```

```
3303
```

Solution to Question 5

6. Write a Python program to remove a key from a dictionary.

```
myDict = {'a':1,'b':2,'c':3,'d':4}
print(myDict)
if 'a' in myDict:
    del myDict['a']
print(myDict)

{'a': 1, 'b': 2, 'c': 3, 'd': 4}
{'b': 2, 'c': 3, 'd': 4}
```

Solution to Question 6

7. Program to create 10 key-value pairs where key is a number in the range 1-10 and the value is twice the number

```
dict={x:2 *x for x in range(1,10)}
print(dict)

{1: 2, 2: 4, 3: 6, 4: 8, 5: 10, 6: 12, 7: 14, 8: 16, 9: 18}
```

Solution to Question 7

8. Program to add a new item in the dictionary

```
dict={'Roll_No' :'IT6001' ,'Name' :'Ishita' ,'Course' :'B.Tech'}
print("dict[Roll_No] = ",dict['Roll_No'])
print("dict[Name] = ", dict['Name'])
print("dict[Course] = " ,dict['Course'])
dict["Marks"]=98
print("dict[Marks] = " ,dict['Marks'])

dict[Roll_No] =  IT6001
dict[Name] =  Ishita
dict[Course] =  B.Tech
dict[Marks] =  98
```

Solution to Question 8

9. Write a program to create nested dictionary

```
Students ={'student1 ' : {'cs':99,'ds': 89 ,'Ec':92} ,'student2' : {'cs':88,'ds':87,'Ec':77} , 'student3': {'cs':91
for key,val in Students.items():
  print(key,val)

student1  {'cs': 99, 'ds': 89, 'Ec': 92}
student2 {'cs': 88, 'ds': 87, 'Ec': 77}
student3 {'cs': 91, 'ds': 92, 'Ec': 88}
```

Solution to Question 9

10.Program to sort keys of a dictionary

```
dict={'Roll_No' :'IT6001' ,'Name' :'Ishita' ,'Course' :'B.Tech'}
print(sorted(dict.keys()))

['Course', 'Name', 'Roll_No']
```

Solution to Question 10

CHAPTER SEVEN

File Handling

1.Write a Python program to read an entire text file

```
def file_read(fname):
        txt = open(fname)
        print(txt.read())

file_read('a.txt')

Python is an interpreted, object-oriented, high-level programming language with dynamic semantics. Its high-level bui
```

Solution to Question 1

2.Write a Python program to read first n lines of a file.

```
def file_read_from_head(fname, nlines):
        from itertools import islice
        with open(fname) as f:
                for line in islice(f, nlines):
                        print(line)
file_read_from_head('a.txt',2)

Python is an interpreted, object-oriented, high-level programming language with dynamic semantics. Its high-level bui
```

Solution to Question 2

3.Write a Python program to append text to a file and display the text.

```
def file_read(fname):
        from itertools import islice
        with open(fname, "w") as myfile:
                myfile.write("Python Exercises\n")
                myfile.write("Data Structure Exercises")
        txt = open(fname)
        print(txt.read())
file_read('a.txt')

Python Exercises
Data Structure Exercises
```

Solution to Question 3

4. Write a Python program to read last n lines of a file.

```
import sys
import os
def file_read_from_tail(fname,lines):
        bufsize = 8192
        fsize = os.stat(fname).st_size
        iter = 0
        with open(fname) as f:
                if bufsize > fsize:
                        bufsize = fsize-1
                        data = []
                        while True:
                                iter +=1
                                f.seek(fsize-bufsize*iter)
                                data.extend(f.readlines())
                                if len(data) >= lines or f.tell() == 0:
                                        print(''.join(data[-lines:]))
                                        break

file_read_from_tail('a.txt',2)


ython Exercises
Data Structure Exercises
```

Solution to Question 4

5. Write a Python program to read a file line by line and store it into a list.

```
def file_read(fname):
        with open(fname) as f:
                #Content_list is the list that contains the read lines.
                content_list = f.readlines()
                print(content_list)

file_read('a.txt')

['Python Exercises\n', 'Data Structure Exercises']
```

Solution to Question 5

6. Write a python program to find the longest words.

```
def longest_word(filename):
    with open(filename, 'r') as infile:
              words = infile.read().split()
    max_len = len(max(words, key=len))
    return [word for word in words if len(word) == max_len]

print(longest_word('a.txt'))


['Exercises', 'Structure', 'Exercises']
```

Solution to Question 6

7.Write a Python program to count the number of lines in a text file.

```
def file_lengthy(fname):
        with open(fname) as f:
                for i, l in enumerate(f):
                        pass
        return i + 1
print("Number of lines in the file: ",file_lengthy("a.txt"))
```

```
Number of lines in the file:  2
```

Solution to Question 7

8.Write a Python program to create a file where all letters of English alphabet are listed by specified number of letters on each line.

```
import string
def letters_file_line(n):
   with open("a.txt", "w") as f:
       alphabet = string.ascii_uppercase
       letters = [alphabet[i:i + n] + "\n" for i in range(0, len(alphabet), n)]
       f.writelines(letters)
   tt=open('a.txt')
   print(tt.read())
letters_file_line(2)
```

```
AB
CD
EF
GH
IJ
KL
MN
OP
QR
ST
UV
WX
YZ
```

Solution to Question 8

9. Count the total number of upper case, lower case, and digits used in the text file “a.txt”.

```
def pro():
    with open("a.txt","r") as f1:
       data=f1.read()
    cnt_ucase =0
    cnt_lcase=0
    cnt_digits=0
    for ch in data:
        if ch.islower():
            cnt_lcase+=1
        if ch.isupper():
            cnt_ucase+=1
        if ch.isdigit():
            cnt_digits+=1
    print("Total Number of Upper Case letters are:",cnt_ucase)
    print("Total Number of Lower Case letters are:",cnt_lcase)
    print("Total Number of  digits are:",cnt_digits)
pro()

Total Number of Upper Case letters are: 26
Total Number of Lower Case letters are: 0
Total Number of  digits are: 0
```

Solution to Question 9

10. Write a function in Python to count words in a text file those are ending with alphabet "e"

```
def count_words():
    file = open("c.txt","r")
    count = 0
    data = file.read()
    words = data.split()
    for word in words:
        if word[-1] == 'e':
            count+=1
    print(count)
    file.close()

count_words()

4
```

Solution to Question 10

9 798887 830148

Printed by Libri Plureos GmbH in Hamburg,
Germany